Food for a Year

The Leading Prepper's Guide to Easily Acquiring, Storing, Stockpiling and Preparing Shelf-Stable Foods for Long-Term Survival (Be Well Prepared for Any Disaster or Emergency!)

By Beau Griffin

Disclaimer

Table of Contents

Introduction

If you've opened this book to find out what it's all about, you're probably asking yourself: why would you need a year's worth of food? That's a question with a very simple answer: because, one day, it might be the difference between life and death for you and your family – and not just in the event of the zombie apocalypse!

Do you have a bank account or retirement account? Most of us do, so let's assume the answer is yes. We save money over our lifetimes both for short term goals and long term needs, and to make sure we are financially secure in the future. We understand instinctively that money is necessary to our quality of life and that it might not always be arriving in our hands at the rate it does right this minute.

That same concept applies to food. It's one of the most basic needs we have as human beings and, along with water and shelter, is something we absolutely cannot live without in a time of disaster.

Preppers know there are plenty of reasons you might find yourself cut off from access to food. Let's start with one that doesn't always get talked about in conversations about prepping for disaster: a crisis in your own life.

It can happen to anyone. The loss of a job, an accident that leaves you unable to work, the death of a spouse or family member, a new financial responsibility, an unexpected cost that wipes out your savings entirely. No matter how well prepared we try to be, we can never completely predict the challenges life is going to throw at us.

If you found yourself in a situation where there was no money coming in and no relief on the horizon, would it not set your heart at rest to know you are sitting on enough food to ensure that you and your family will not go hungry? A year is a long time to recover from a personal crisis, and knowing you have the basics cover can make it much easier to bounce back.

Traditionally, of course, preppers have worked to be ready for more widespread disasters. This could be anything from a short-term incident like a winter storm or hurricane to a period of civil unrest that makes it dangerous to go out on the streets or an invasion from another country. It could also be a long term disaster, including a widespread famine that makes food scarce, a nuclear war or a pandemic spreading through the population.

Take a look at the history books and the news of even the recent past and you'll see that any of these scenarios are possible. They come out of the blue to devastate life as we know it, and suddenly it's extremely difficult to ensure the safety of your family.

But it doesn't have to be, and that's what prepping is all about. It's about making sure you have the basic needs covered, no matter what may happen. It's an investment for your future just like your bank account or retirement savings. It's a way to make use of what you have available now to protect your future and ensure that, no matter what happens, you're in the strongest possible position to survive it.

The Elements of a Healthy Diet

Before you can start putting together a year's worth of food for yourself and your dependents, it's important to have an understanding of what exactly you are going to need. Obviously, when you're selecting your pantry items, the most important fact about a food is going to be its ability to stay viable over a long period. However, its ability to keep you healthy and hearty is also vital.

To stay healthy, you're going to need numerous macro and micro nutrients. It's a good idea to research the exact levels you need for your sex, age, height, weight and health requirements, and do the same for anyone else your pantry is going to need. This cumulative total will help you make decisions about types of food and quantities when the time comes to stock your pantry.

Macro Nutrients

Protein

This macro nutrient is arguably the most important of all of them, as it is the building block used by your body to create new cells and repair itself. Your body is not capable of making the amino acids it needs for this purpose on its own, which is why you need to get them from your food.

The majority of people get protein from meats and dairy products – fortunately, there are long term storage options that will make this possible in your pantry. There are also additional sources that will keep well over time, including seeds, nuts and beans. It's impossible to stress strongly enough how important it is to make sure protein features prominently in your long term pantry – without it, you won't stay healthy for very long.

Fiber

This nutrient is the "odd one out" because you don't actually absorb or use it. Instead, your body uses it to keep your digestion going, helping the system keep moving and ensuring your gut health. It's important to make sure you're getting enough as there are medical issues associated with a lack of fiber in the diet.

Carbohydrates

This macro nutrient is an energy source. Whether it's simple sugar or more complex whole wheats, carbs will ultimately end up broken down by the body and converted into energy for the body to use. Obviously, your body is going to need an appropriate amount of carbs each day to keep functioning properly.

Fats

Fats are also used for energy, but they also have other purposes. They are important, for example, for the health of your joints, hair and nails. They help you absorb vitamins – A, D, E and K are, in fact, known as the "fat-soluble vitamins". They contain essential fatty acids that your body is not able to make and that are used for brain development, inflammation control and blood clotting.

Some fats are better than others – saturated fats such as butter, cheese and ice cream will raise your bad cholesterol levels, for example – but that may not be something you can control as easily during a time when you are relying on long term storage. Getting your fats in whatever manner possible is your priority.

Micro Nutrients

This category includes all the vitamins and minerals the body needs on a daily basis. Below is a list of the vital ones and the average daily quantity recommended by the

FDA for an adult. This may not exactly match your personal needs, of course, so use it only as a general guideline as you start thinking about your pantry:

Vitamins

- Biotin, 30 mcg – Used for energy storage and metabolism support.
- Choline, 550 mg – Used for brain development, cell signaling, fat metabolism, liver function, muscle movement, nerve function.
- Folic Acid, 400 mcg – Used for red blood cell formation and metabolism.
- Niacin, 16 mg – Used for digestion, nervous system function, production of cholesterol and converting food into energy.
- Pantothenic Acid, 5 mg – Used for hormone production, nervous system function, red blood cell formation and fat metabolism.
- Riboflavin, 1.3 mg – Used to convert food into energy, for growth and development and for red blood cell formation.
- Thiamin, 1.2 mg – Used to convert food into energy and for nervous system function.
- Vitamin A, 900 mcg – Used for growth and development, immune function, red blood cell formation, reproduction, skin and bone formation and vision.

- Vitamin B6, 1.7 mg – Used for immune function, nervous system function, metabolism and red blood cell formation.
- Vitamin B12, 2.4 mcg – Used to convert food into energy and for nervous system function and red blood cell formation.
- Vitamin C, 90 mg – Used as an antioxidant, for the formation of collagen and connective tissue, for immune function and for wound healing.
- Vitamin D, 20 mcg (or more) – Used to regulate blood pressure, for bone growth, for calcium balance, for hormone production, for immune function and for nervous system function.
- Vitamin E, 15 mg – Used as an antioxidant, for the formation of blood vessels and for immune function.
- Vitamin K, 120 mcg – Used for blood clotting and strong bones.

Minerals

- Calcium, 1300 mg (or more) – Used for blood clotting, bone and teeth formation, blood vessel support, hormone secretion, muscle contraction and nervous system function.
- Chloride, 2300 mg – Used for acid base balance, conversion of food into energy, digestion, fluid balance and nervous system function.

- Chromium, 35 mcg – Used for insulin function and metabolism
- Copper, 0.9 mg – Used as an antioxidant, for bone formation, for collagen and connective tissue formation, for energy production, for iron metabolism and for nervous system function.
- Iodine, 150 mcg – Used for growth and development, metabolism, reproduction and thyroid hormone production.
- Iron, 18 mg (or more) – Used for energy production, growth and development, immune function, red blood cell formation, reproduction and wound healing.
- Magnesium, 420 mg – Used to regulate blood pressure and blood sugar, for bone formation, for energy production, for hormone secretion, for immune function, for muscle contraction, for nervous system function, for a normal heart rhythm and for protein formation.
- Molybdenum, 45 mcg – Used for enzyme production.
- Phosphorus, 1250 mg – Used for acid-based balance, bone formation, energy production and storage and hormone activation.
- Potassium, 4700 mg (or more) – Used for blood pressure regulation, metabolism, fluid balance, growth and development, heart function, muscle

contraction, nervous system function and protein
formation.

- Selenium, 55 mcg – Used as an antioxidant, for
  immune function, for reproduction and for thyroid
  function.
- Sodium, 2300 mg (or less) – Used for acid base
  balance, blood pressure regulation, fluid balance,
  muscle contraction and nervous system function.
- Zinc, 11 mg – Used for growth and development,
  immune function, nervous system function, protein
  formation, reproduction, taste and smell and
  wound healing.

As you can see from this list, the human diet is
complicated and interactive. Each of the elements you eat
works in tandem with the others to keep you functioning
properly, and to support all the different systems that
make up your body.

It's a long list and a detailed one, but that only serves to
underline the point: when putting together your pantry,
you need to bear in mind exactly what nutrients you'll be
getting.

There are certain food types that are great for keeping
your micro nutrients coming. Whole grains, for instant,
contain biotin, niacin, pantothenic acid, thiamin,
chromium, copper, iron, magnesium, manganese,

phosphorus, molybdenum, selenium and zinc. That's a lot of necessary nutrients ticked off your list with just one ingredient on your pantry shelf.

That's why, as you start planning your pantry, it's important to keep an eye on not only the financial side and how long the food can be stored, but also the ingredients you choose and how well they will support your health.

How Much Food Will You Need?

"A year's supply" is something of an ephemeral concept. Can you simply multiply your weekly groceries by 52 and work on that basis? Not really, because the types of food you'll be working with, and how you'll divide your pantry between the necessary nutrients, is very different from the average weekly grocery list.

A supply of food for one year is also going to look different for a child to how it looks for an adult. Fortunately, there's an easy way to calculate your needs, because expert preppers have already done the work on your behalf.

Below, you will find the total amount of each type of food that you will need for each person your pantry is going to feed. You'll find one chart for adults, and a second for any children under the age of around 7 who will be sheltering with you. Simply multiply these figures by the number of adults and children in your group to calculate the totals of each pantry ingredient you're going to need.

Adults

Grains

Total: 390 lbs

Split between: 200 lbs of wheat, 70 lbs of rice, 30 lbs of flour, 30 lbs of oats, 30 lbs of pasta, 30 lbs of corn meal.

Canned and Dried Meats

Total: 20 lbs

(Note that dehydrated and freeze dried meat weighs approximately one third of the amount of normal meat.)

Fats and Oils

Total: 25 lbs

Split between: 2 gallons of vegetable oil, 4 lbs of shortening, 1 quart of salad dressing, 2 quarts of mayonnaise, 4 lbs of peanut butter.

Beans and Legumes

Total: 70 lbs

Split between: 40 lbs of dry beans, 10 lbs of soy beans, 5 lbs of lima beans, 5 lbs of split peas, 5 lbs of lentils, 5 lbs of dry soup mix.

Milk and Dairy

Total: 87 lbs

Split between: 72 lbs of dry milk, 15 cans of evaporated milk, 15 lbs of other dairy.

Sugars

Total: 60 lbs

Split between: 40 lbs of sugar, 3 lbs of brown sugar, 3 lbs of honey, 3 lbs of jams, 1 lb of corn syrup, 1 lb of molasses, 6 lbs of powdered juice mix, 1 lb of jello mix.

Cooking Essentials

Salt: 5 lbs
Baking powder: 1 lb
Baking soda: 1 lb
Yeast: 1 lb
Vinegar: 1 gallon

Fruits and Vegetables

Total Canned: 320 quarts

Total Dried: 90 lbs

Water

Total: 183 gallons

(Plus one gallon of bleach, used at a dilution of 8-16 drops per gallon of water for sanitation.)

Children

Grains

Total: 195 lbs

Split between: 100 lbs of wheat, 35 lbs of rice, 27 lbs of flour, 27 lbs of oats, 27 lbs of pasta, 27 lbs of corn meal.

Canned and Dried Meats

Total: 10 lbs

Fats and Oils

Total: 13 lbs

Split between: 1 gallon of vegetable oil, 2 lbs of shortening, 1 quart of salad dressing, 1 quart of mayonnaise, 2 lbs of peanut butter.

Beans and Legumes

Total: 35 lbs

Split between: 20 lbs of dry beans, 5 lbs of soy beans, 3 lbs of lima beans, 3 lbs of split peas, 3 lbs of lentils, 3 lbs of dry soup mix.

Milk and Dairy

Total: 44 lbs

Split between: 45 lbs of dry milk, 8 cans of evaporated milk, 8 lbs of other dairy.

Sugars

Total: 30 lbs

Split between: 20 lbs of sugar, 2 lbs of brown sugar, 2 lbs of honey, 2 lbs of jams, 1 lb of corn syrup, 1 lb of molasses, 3 lbs of powdered juice mix, 1 lb of jello mix.

Cooking Essentials

Salt: 3 lbs
Baking powder: 1 lb
Baking soda: 1 lb
Yeast: 1 lb
Vinegar: 1 gallon

Fruits and Vegetables

Total Canned: 160 quarts

Total Dried: 45 lbs

Water

Total: 92 gallons

(Plus half a gallon of bleach, used at a dilution of 8-16 drops per gallon of water for sanitation.)

Spreading Out the Cost

The idea of buying a year's worth of food is undoubtedly a daunting one. That's a lot of money to sink into something that you're hoping never to have to use.

Later in the book, we will be looking at how to make use of your pantry so that you are cycling items out before they reach their expiry date and never wasting your investment. But to do that, you need a stocked pantry, which means you need to start the process of adding to it.

A New Mindset

This is going to require a new mindset when it comes to grocery shopping. You are not going to purchase an entire year's worth of food at one time; rather, you will be embarking on an ongoing process that will remain a work in progress until such time your pantry is needed.

You may already have this mindset if you're the kind of person who likes to buy in bulk because you know it's cheaper, or purchase extras of items that are temporarily less expensive than usual. The good news is that prepping a year long pantry is just an expansion of this mindset, which also means you'll have the chance to expand on some of those savings.

Yes, a year's worth of food is expensive. On the other hand, think of it as an opportunity to purchase extra bags of rice or jars of peanut butter when you see them on offer or at a lower price. If that doesn't tickle your fancy because, in your imagination, it will simply be disappearing into a dark storage room, never to be seen again until the worst happens, remember that you are going to be cycling your food.

That rice is going to come back out to be used by the family before it expires. It is, in fact, an item in your regular pantry…just not yet.

Bargain Hunting

Your grocery shopping trips are going to be more focused than ever on looking for bargains and searching out items that will store for a long time at a good price. Over time, your long term pantry will grow into a supply that will keep you safe for a day, but there's no need to go out today and try to purchase everything you need.

It's a good idea to start keeping notes of price points for the kinds of ingredients you'll be storing. Update your notes with the lowest price you've found so far for each item, so you can tell at a glance while at the grocery store whether you're really getting a bargain.

It's also worth adding some variety to your shopping routine. Instead of sticking to the same store each time, choose a different one each week. Try to find four or five that are local enough to you and cycle around them over the month.

That way, you'll be able to price check the items on your pantry list at each business on a regular basis and you're more likely to find the good prices. Over time, you'll start to figure out the timing of sales in each store, where to go to find the cheapest versions of the ingredients you need and whether to purchase a bulk item in one store or the same item individually elsewhere – the prices really can be different enough to matter.

Your Stockpile

The next step of the mindset is to stop thinking about "the week's groceries" and start thinking about your stockpile. This, of course, applies only to the items you intend to keep in your store, and not the meats, dairy and fresh produce you are buying for the week's meals.

The first part of this is to locate one of your pantry staples at a good price, as we talked about above, and with a long expiry date. Let's say it's rice. You know already how much of it you will need to feed each person in your group for a full year, so you know the maximum necessary for your pantry.

White rice has an average expiry date around four years, so it's not an ingredient you need to cycle quickly. You can therefore feel safe to purchase any quantity up to the amount you would want to store in your year long pantry, even if you wouldn't normally use that much in the space of 12 months.

(As a side note, this is one reason it's very important to look for the longest expiry dates possible. In a time of crisis, you are almost certainly going to be eating far more of the long life ingredients in your pantry than you would at any other time. That means you're not going to be able to cycle out a year's worth of canned meat in the space of a year – even with changes to your diet, it will take you longer than that. This needs to be factored in when making shopping choices; while building your pantry, don't invest in more of a particular ingredient than you can actually eat before its expiry date.)

Purchase your rice in bulk, taking advantage of the excellent price, and add it to your pantry stockpile. Purchase as much as you can justify with your budget. You can then start using the rice from your stockpile and replace it the next time you find a bargain, preferably in a larger quantity than the amount you've used in the meantime so that your stockpile continues to grow until it reaches the right amount to last you for a year.

Starting the Cycle

You might already have figured out that you're going to need to start making some changes to your daily diet. While you do have a great deal of leeway in terms of choosing items for your year long pantry that you enjoy eating, you're still going to have to start building all of your chosen ingredients into your regular diet.

You are going to need to do so regularly enough that you can maintain the cycling process. Let's say, for example, that right now you don't eat any canned beans at all, but you will need to include them in your pantry for the nutrients. Let's say that you've found beans with an expiry date four years from now and added them to your pantry.

To be sure that all your beans are still edible when the time comes to actually use your pantry, you're going to need to have eaten every can you've purchased within four years. That means you'll need to eat a quarter of them per year and will have to factor that into your meal planning.

As you can see, because most long term foods have a longer expiry than a year, you're not going to be stuck eating a long term pantry diet from here on out. But you are going to need to select foods for your pantry that you can build into your normal diet, and you are going to need to make some alterations to that diet.

You can also see by now that starting your stockpile is not as daunting as it seemed. It's easier to stomach smaller purchases on a weekly basis than forking out your savings on a full year's worth of food.

Building Your Supplies

There are other ways to build your stockpile, of course. For example, if you receive a lump sum of money, such as an inheritance or a bonus or a birthday gift or a win in a raffle, consider using at least a portion of it towards your pantry. You know now that you are investing in your future in more than one way: you're not only future proofing your family's food stores, you're also taking advantage of bargain prices for a significant portion of your normal grocery shopping. That makes stockpiling an excellent use of your windfall.

If you are keen to get started fast and have enough food in your pantry to last for a few months as quickly as you can, but that's far outside the possibilities of your budget, consider a yard sale or using social media to get rid of some of your belongings that you don't need any more. Use that money to kick start your storage, giving yourself the peace of mind that you can already survive for a period of time if the worst happens.

Watch out for coupons – these can save you considerable money, especially if you use them on sale items. Many will be for non food items, such as shampoo and soap. These are items you would also need in an emergency situation, so they're also worth making use of.

See if there are any food co-ops in your area. Through these, groups of people purchase food in bulk and distribute it among themselves, taking advantage together of the fact that the higher the quantity, the lower the price will usually be. If the co-op is for fresh items, don't discount it – you could consider canning or preserve them.

On a similar note, look for discard items at the end of the day in a farmer's market or supermarket. The seller will usually discard the less appealing items or the ones that are unlikely to sell the next day, and will do so at extremely good prices. These can be preserved, dehydrated or used in ingredients such as a tomato sauce that can then be stored long term.

There's also a lot to be said for creating your own food to store. A lot of fruits and vegetables can be stored long term in some way, so why not start your own garden right away? Focus on items that can be stored. As you harvest your beans, squash, tomatoes, peas and other items, you can simply can or preserve them and add them to your pantry.

The same goes for hunting. While it will cost you a certain amount of money for equipment, license fees and other necessities, you have the opportunity to harvest a whole animal for your pantry. Some of this can be made into jerky or cured and will be perfect for your year long pantry; the rest can replace purchased meat in your freezer, freeing up some cash to direct towards your pantry instead.

Budgeting for a Stockpile

These ideas will all help, but your best overall approach as you continue the process of stockpiling will be to reconsider your personal budget. Take a look at your monthly expenses as they stand right now and consider whether there are any items you could cut out without really missing them. Decide if there are luxury or entertainment purchases you don't really need to make, for example. Once you have done this, you will be able to mark out a monthly amount that can go towards building your stockpile. Again, keep in mind that all of this food is going to be used – all you are doing is working to build a much bigger store room than you've had in the past.

Use this monthly budget when you spot sales and bargains – that's the best way to build a frugal pantry that will save you money in the long term. Once your pantry is complete, you will start reaping the benefits of all that bargain hunting – and everything new you put in there will also be at the best possible price you can find.

Finding the Right Storage Space

There's no way around it: a year's supply of food is going to take up some serious space. It's important to figure out exactly where that space is going to be as quickly as possible, not only to make it easier to maintain an inventory (and to prevent an avalanche of tins falling through the kitchen door every time you open it), but to ensure your food lasts as long as possible.

You're going to need a dedicated storage area – but not just any old space. The best long term pantries are able to preserve your food for the longest possible time simply by maintaining the right balance of such things as light and moisture.

Choosing a Space

The things you will be looking for as you make your choice include:

Location: You need your food storage to be in close proximity to the home in which you would be sheltering if disaster struck. That may mean it needs to be in or near your current house, or it could mean it's located in the basement of a remote cabin you intend to take your family to. Making sure it's close at hand is important not only for ease of access, but also so that you can be present as much as possible to ensure it is protected. Choosing a location that is less obvious is also a good idea, again to protect against theft. If your food storage isn't obvious, there's a better chance a home invader would miss it. For this reason, you may also want to consider a second, back up storage space, such as in a buried weatherproof container or at your vacation cabin. If the worst happens, whether that be damage to your food stores or a home invader, you will have an emergency supply.

Light: Sunlight is not your friend when it comes to storage. Your long term pantry should be dark for as much of the day as possible, which means either choosing a space without windows or blocking them to keep the light out.

Temperature: The cooler you can keep your storage space, the better. For this reason, the best places for a year long pantry are usually below ground level, such as in cellars and basements, or even root cellars. Your attic might be the most open space in your house, but it's not a great choice for a pantry because it will be one of the warmest parts of your house. If you have no space inside, consider your garage or even a camping trailer. High temperatures are not your only enemy when it comes to food – fluctuations are also a problem when it comes to shelf life, so you don't want to choose a space that is served by your home's heating system. It is, of course, possible to create these conditions above ground, though it's harder. It's not recommended that you use air conditioning to keep your food pantry cool simply because, if you are in a position where you need to make use of your storage, your air conditioning might well not be working.

Moisture: You want to prevent your food items from becoming damp at all costs. Make sure your chosen area does not suffer from damp in the cooler months, does not flood in winter and spring and is not naturally humid. If there is any danger of flooding, use pallets to raise your storage off the floor. This is also a good idea if your floor is concrete, which can cause condensation when a can is placed directly on it.

Rodents and Insects: Mice, rats and other pests will not only steal some of your food, they will also contaminate what they leave behind. Even if you don't believe there is likely to be a problem in your storage area, don't count out these pests – they have a way of getting exactly where they are wanted least. Use the relevant traps for both rodents and insects within your storage area at all times. This will not only protect your food, but also give you early warning if pests have found your stash. After all, as the wise have always said, when you see one mouse, there are ten more nearby that you aren't seeing.

Shelving Options

Once you've chosen your storage space, it's time to transform it into a pantry. You have three main considerations at this point. First, you want to be able to store as much as you can in the space you have available. Second, you want it to be organized so that you know exactly where to find the things you need. And thirdly, you want to be able to incorporate a rotation system right from the start, making it easy to take a trip to your pantry to add new items and remove the old ones.

That means shelving – and plenty of it. It also means sturdy shelving, because your stored food is going to be heavy. Wood or heavy duty metal is best – this is not an element of your project on which you can skimp, because a buckled shelf is going to cause a lot of damage and ultimately cost you a pretty penny.

To protect your food from earthquakes, explosions and other events that could shake the room, or even from shoulders, elbows and box edges as you move things in and out of the space, be sure that your shelving units have been properly secured to the wall. If you also have shelving in the middle of the room, secure it to the ceiling and floor.

For the same reason, it's a good idea to line your shelves with non slip rubber to make sure boxes and jars don't slide around. You can also purchase shelves with a protective strip or lip that stops items from tumbling over the edge. Breakable items such as jars can be stored in boxes.

Lots of thinner shelves are usually better than a small number of wide shelves, simply because you'll find it easier to see what items are in your storage – and access them. You should also vary the height of your shelves to accommodate larger items such as buckets as well as smaller items like cans.

Designing Your Organization System

You need to know what's in your pantry at all times and you need to be able to tell which items are ready to be rotated out. It would be easy for a task like this to take over your life, costing you many hours of checking sell by dates every time you visit the grocery store, but it doesn't have to. That's where your organization system comes in.

The first and most vital rule of an organization system is that foods of a specific type will always be stored with the newest item at the back and the oldest near the front. This will mean that you only need pick up the nearest can or jar to see its use by date and determine that it's time to replace it with something new.

The rest of your organization system will depend on what works for your own personality, available space and needs. You could, for example, organize by food type, keeping all your meats on one shelf, all your vegetables on another and so on. This would mean that your foods in one category would sit together regardless of how they are stored, so a can of green beans from your garden will sit next to a freeze dried package of beans. The advantage of this system is that you will be able to find foods fast and know immediately that you are running low on a particular type of item. It will also make unpacking very easy, because you have specific spots for everything. However, it will mean you need more uniform shelving and all of your shelving will need to be large enough to accommodate the biggest storage type you plan to use. If your storage area is relatively small, this could prove to be a waste of valuable space.

Alternatively, you could organize according to the type of container your foods are stored in. One area of your pantry would be for jars, for example, another for cans and yet another for buckets. This does not have the same advantage of making it easy to find what you are looking for, but it does maximize your available space because it is easier to stack your food and prevent wasted space. You could also improve your ability to find things quickly in this style of organization by color coding types of food and labeling each item accordingly as you add it.

Other options include organizing alphabetically, which carries the same advantages as putting like items together and also similar downsides. You could also place the most used foods closest to the door and the least used at the far end, or divide your pantry according to meal types: breakfast, lunch, dinner, snacks and miscellaneous. You could also organize by meal planning, placing everything you require for a specific meal you often make in one place. You could even place every item you need for a single meal into a sack or box, which you can simply grab and go.

Rotating Your Stock

We've mentioned this before and we will likely mention it again, because it's the cornerstone of a successful long term pantry. Rotating your food items in and out of storage is vital to ensuring you're in the best possible position when you need to make use of your pantry. It's also going to ensure that all the money you are investing in your pantry is never wasted.

Do you need to make sure every item on the shelf has an expiration date at least a year out? Preferably, yes, if only because the situation you find yourself might last longer than a year and you could find yourself needing to stretch your supplies out while shoring them up with such things as home grown vegetables.

As you start growing your stores, however, this is not going to be your uppermost concern. Right now, you just want to be able to fill your pantry with a year's worth of food. Bear in mind that, if disaster happens and you need to start using your pantry, you aren't going to eat every single food item in your year's supply on day 365. If you have some items at the front of your shelves that will only last six months, all you need do is make sure you choose to eat them first.

The more robust your pantry becomes, the more you will want to work on adding items that will last as long as possible. This will also become easier as you get into the habit of incorporating your long term foods into your regular daily diet.

Ideally, you want to get into the routine of checking your pantry every time you go grocery shopping. Items that are about to drop below your longevity limit can be transferred to your regular pantry, and replacements can be added to your grocery list. This will mean changing the habits of a lifetime but, after a while, it will become second nature.

There's also a tool that will help you with this task…

Making Your Master Inventory

Your master inventory is a document that contains records of every item of food you have stored, when it expires and what quantities are currently available. That sounds simple, but it does require ongoing maintenance to ensure your inventory is up to date.

Like most things related to preparing for a disaster scenario, it's not necessarily a good idea to use electronics to create your master list. In this case, however, you can very easily make it work.

Create a spreadsheet separated into sections according to the method by which you've organized your pantry (type of food, type of storage etc.). Create columns for the name of the food, the quantity of it you require for the whole family for one year and the quantity you have available. Use the equation function to have the spreadsheet use the next column to calculate the exact amount of that food you still need to purchase for your storage to be complete. In column 5, enter the nearest sell-by date for your collection of that food item; column six will be the quantity of food with that closest sell-by date.

You can also include notes on your spreadsheet with information about such things as where you bought it, what bargain price you found, even where it is in your pantry, if you wish.

Every time you add or remove items from your pantry, update this spreadsheet. You will then want to print it out and keep a hard copy inside the pantry itself, readily available if and when you need to start using your long term storage.

A spreadsheet program on your computer is the easiest and neatest way to achieve this, but you can of course go the old fashioned route and draw up a spreadsheet by hand. Either way, you will still be able to check it when it comes time for grocery shopping to see what items you still need to look for and which items are ready to replace.

It's entirely your choice, but do always make sure you will be able to access your spreadsheet easily when you need it

– and make sure to keep it up to date so you can feel confident that you know exactly what food is on hand at all times.

How to Store Your Food

Some of the food items you'll be stockpiling in your pantry will come in containers that are already ideal. Jars and cans, for example, will protect the food inside from going bad by keeping it sealed, air tight and protected from outside contaminants.

Some packaging, however, is not designed for long term storage, and oxygen is not your friend when it comes to keeping food fresh. Nor is a disaster such as flooding or earthquake, which can destroy packaging very easily and expose your food to contaminants.

A good rule of thumb when it comes to choosing food storage items is to always bear in mind your rotation system. Wherever possible, you want to be able to rotate usable quantities in and out of your storage.

The secret to an easy pantry is to make use of your storage solutions in such a way that you can add and remove single portions at a time. (By portions, we mean sufficient for everyone in your household for a single meal). This is not as difficult as it seems.

You will want to focus on the following storage solutions in your pantry:

Jars and Cans: Food that comes in this type of packaging can be left alone and stored as you bought it, as long as you don't break the seals or puncture the lid or can. Most grocery store bought items of this kind already come in portion sizes, which means that this part of your pantry is the very easiest to maintain. You can also purchase empty cans and jars and the appropriate equipment to seal them properly, which will allow you to can and jar your own produce for long term storage. Bear in mind that jars are highly breakable, so it's a good idea to run a thin board across the front of shelves to keep them from falling.

5-gallon Buckets: We recommend opting for gamma lids for these, as they are much easier to open and seal the bucket more thoroughly. Look for buckets that stack well. Check in with your local grocery store – they often receive food in these buckets and simply throw them out, so they may let you take them for free or a nominal price. Some items can simply be stored inside these buckets and the whole thing can be rotated in and out of the pantry. A bucket will hold, for example, 5 lbs of wheat or 2.5 lbs of oats or 5.3 lbs of rice or 5.7 lbs of sugar, and is therefore ideal for loose items of this kind. If you wish, you can also use the sealed bucket to fortify the packaging of other items. For instance, we mentioned that cereal packets are not completely air tight. Instead of emptying them from the box, simply keep the boxes stored inside your 5-gallon bucket. This will also provide protection

Mylar Bags: The beauty of these bags is that they come in all sorts of shapes and sizes, each one capable of protecting your food. Smaller bags are ideal to seal small amounts or individual portions, which means you won't have to follow the process of removing the oxygen every time. You will also need a bag sealer, which will suck the oxygen from the package and inhibit the growth of bacteria or hatching of bug eggs. Mylar bags inside buckets is the golden standard for food storage, because the bags will protect against oxygen and humidity while the bucket protects against physical damage and adds an extra layer of oxygen and humidity control.

These are your main tools for storage, but you do still have other options if you need them, whether for awkwardly sized items or cost. You can reuse plastic bottles, such as soda bottles, to store things like sugar or beans. Before use, clean it thoroughly and disinfect before letting it dry thoroughly. Make sure the bottle has the plastic PET triangle on the bottom.

Tupperware and other sealable plastic containers are also extremely handy, and can often be bought in large sets that will stack well. Both of these options should only be used for six months or less, however, as plastic will always eventually leach into the food.

Preparing Food in Emergency Situations

There is a strong likelihood that a situation in which you need to rely on food storage for an extended period of time is also a situation where you are lacking in basic utilities. If you lose electricity, you also use the ability to use your stove, microwave and other kitchen items.

There's not much point having a year's worth of food sitting in your basement if you have no way to prepare it, so it's important to plan ahead for this part of the process, too. Consider choosing one or more of the following options to either add to your household right now or keep in storage for when it is needed:

Outside Grill: You'll obviously need a supply of propane tanks for this to work, but this is an effective and easy way to cook in an emergency. You can even use it to bake, by preheating it and then placing your item inside and sealing the lid.

Camping or Butane Stove: This is a lot like a traditional stovetop, which means you can cook anything on it that you would usually cook in a pan or skillet. You will need to use a camping stove outside because it emits carbon monoxide. A butane stove is usually safer to use inside, but it's worth investing in a carbon monoxide detector just in case.

Fire Pit: You can build one of these in the yard to cook over and add a grate to the top so that you can grill, use a Dutch oven or heat in a pan. It's easy, as well as being cheap as long as you can access wood easily.

Wood Stove: Installing this in your home not only means you have an emergency cooking solution, it also gives you a heating source for your house right away. Look for models that allow you to bake in it as well as cook on top. Always make sure you have a year's worth of fuel stored at your house, if possible.

HERC Oven: This is an oven powered by small candles, or tea lights. This can be used for baked goods.

Solar Oven: Weather permitting, you can use an oven powered only by the sun. This is less useful in the winter time, but a potentially useful investment if you live in an area with an appropriate climate.

To cook your food, of course, you will also need to prepare your food, and that means you're going to need tools. Many of these may already be present in your kitchen, but it's worth checking the list to be sure:

- Manual can opener
- Set of kitchen knives
- Hand utensils including servings spoons, spatulas, rolling pin, cheese grater, whisk
- Egg beaters
- Measuring cups
- Grain grinder (hand crank)
- Hand chopper
- Coffee grinder (hand crank)
- Cutlery and dishware
- Water filter
- Roasting pans
- Tea kettle
- Colanders
- Cookie sheets
- Saucepans (cast iron or durable stainless steel if cooking over a wood stove)
- Matches and firelighters

Any of these items that do not fit into your usual kitchen equipment list can be stored in your pantry for use when needed. Consider when looking at what you already have that you will be cooking in a different way if the power goes out, so you should make sure your utensils, pans and baking equipment is durable enough and of the right

material to work in whichever cooking situation you have
available.

Taking an Initial Inventory

Before you start purchasing anything for your stockpile, you need to know what you already have. That sentence might have been startling, because you may not have automatically assumed that your current food storage has anything to do with your year long supply.

Through the chapters you've read so far, though, you've gotten a basic idea of the cyclical nature of long term stockpiles. Food doesn't just disappear into your basement, never to be seen again – you'll be bringing food out and replacing it on a regular basis.

That means you already have the beginnings of a long term storage – and it's waiting for you in your current pantry.

This step should be taken as soon as you've completed the preparations in your long term storage and have decided on the organizational system you need. You'll also need to have prepared your spreadsheet, because you're about to start updating those quantities.

It's spring cleaning time. Your first task is to pull out every single food item in the house (except from the fridge and ONLY from the freezer if you will have a generator available to power it if the electricity goes out. If you remove items from the freezer, do so only for long enough to write down its name and quantity).

Now sort your food items into categories, preferably according to the organizational system you've chosen for your pantry. Enter items and quantities into your spreadsheet. These items are the beginnings of your storage, because they are items that would be available right now if you needed to start relying on your long term stores.

Look for any items you already own in quantities that will last longer than the typical time between grocery store visits (a week, a fortnight – however often you usually go). This is often the case for things like rice, flour and baking supplies. Any excess over the amount you will likely use between now and your next grocery shop can already be transported down to your pantry.

From now on, aim wherever practical to only to keep the supply of food you need between grocery visits in your kitchen cupboards – everything else is going down into your stores. This will make things simpler when rotating your food in and out of the long term pantry.

Why is this an important first step? Now that you have some items in your long term pantry, you can see which areas are fuller and which are more bare. You have a good idea of how long your current stores would last you if you lost access to the outside world right now and where the most important gaps are.

This will help you decide where to place your focus when you start purchasing items to place in your long term store. For instance, you may have gone through a recent phase of baking every day and have a large amount of sugar, flour and shortening. On the other hand, you only have a couple of cans of vegetables in the cupboard. Looking at your store, you can instantly see that buying vegetables will be more of a priority than more flour.

*****

Before we continue, I have a small favor to ask:

Could you please take a minute of your time to write an honest review of the book?

Your reviews are what keeps me going. I read every single one of them, and would be **extremely thankful** if you choose to share your thoughts with me.

*****

Stockpiling Food

At this point, you know how much food you are going to need per person in your household, you know what kinds of food are necessary and you are aware of what you have in stock already and have a plan for purchasing the rest. What comes next is to start your food collection.

Over the next weeks and months, you will be gradually adding to your stores until you have a pantry that can feed your party for a year. Until now, we've taken a high level view of the actual foods you will want to have in storage, so it's time to dive a little deeper into the best food choices for your long term health and wellbeing in the event that you can no longer go to a grocery store.

Use these next chapters to make some decisions about what foods you want to store. Everyone has different tastes when it comes to mealtimes, even for the most basic of ingredients, and you have plenty of options to help you whittle down the possibilities into a set of foods that wouldn't just serve you well through an emergency situation, but can also be incorporated into your everyday meal plans to make sure you keep your stock rotated.

With your totals in hand, browse the following chapters, making notes as you go. Your aim is to fill out each aspect of your storage needs chart with ideas of what foods you would prefer to eat. It's probably a good idea to double check your choices with the rest of your household once you're done, just to be sure you will all have plenty of food that you can enjoy.

Protein

This particular nutrient comes largely from meats, but is also found in nuts, beans and a few other places. As the building block of your health, it's a vital part of your food storage, so what kind of options are available in a long term storage situation?

Meats

Canned Meats: Probably the easiest choice, partly because it only needs to be placed on a shelf in the can you bought it in and partly because of the wide variety of options. You'll find everything from chicken, bacon, beef and pork to seafood such as pilchards, salmon and tuna. You will also find processed meats such as Spam and corned beef, as well as meats that have been prepared into meals such as soup, chili and ravioli. Most of these will last up to five years on the shelf, which is great news for your rotation cycle. However, they are nowhere near as popular a pantry staple as fresh and frozen meats, which means you might not be used to cooking with them. If that's the case, consider buying a few of the locally available options and including them in a meal before you make decisions about which you'll find the most appealing. It's also wise to be aware that many canned meats are highly processed, which is best avoided wherever possible.

Dried Meat: Jerky is the ever popular family snack, and that will still be the case during a lockdown situation. However, its shelf life is usually only up to about 18 months, so check the packaging carefully and be prepared to cycle it in and out of your pantry more often than other types of meat. It's also not the easiest food to include in a main meal, which means it won't be your go-to choice for dinners. However, it's an extremely easy way to make sure your family is getting the protein it needs and keep the hunger pangs away at the same time.

Frozen Meat: This option is risky. If you will have access to a generator during an emergency situation, you are able to hook that generator up to your freezer and you are confident that you have sufficient fuel to keep it running (and no more pressing needs it could be used for), then you can use a vacuum sealer to extend the shelf life of frozen meats to up to five years. All is not lost if you do lose access to power, as long as you do still have access to canning and drying equipment (or if you live in a colder part of the world with plenty of snowfall in winter, in which case you can pack down your frozen goods into the snow – although your power is still going to need to last through the warmer months), but this is still a type of protein to think about very carefully before you invest. On the plus side, it opens up your cooking opportunities considerably, because freshly frozen pork, beef, turkey, bacon, sausage, chicken and lamb is the mainstay of most kitchens. If unsure, consider aiming to have enough frozen meats to include in your diet every so often as a treat.

Freeze Dried Meat: These are meats that have been flash frozen and sealed in a vacuum ready for you to rehydrate later. Once prepared, they don't taste much different to fresh meat. This is a more expensive option, but in many ways a better one, than canned or frozen meats. This is not only due to its flavor, which is both appealing and similar to what you'd expect from that type of meat, but also due to its storage time. Freeze dried meats will last up to 25 years, which seriously reduces the amount of cycling you'll need to do.

As well as purchasing meats that have already been packaged in these forms, you can supplement your stores by preparing your own. For example, you can dry your own jerky and seal it up for storage.

Curing Meats

You can also cure your own meats, a technique that involves preserving it in salt. It's a historical method that was used to keep meat fresh before fridges were invented, and is still popular today due to the enhanced taste. It's great for fish, beef and particularly pork.

Curing meats is a method that focuses on the water in the meat, which bacteria need if they're going to thrive. The salt expels a lot of this water and makes the meat more inhospitable for that bacteria.

For around ten to 12 pounds of meat, you'll need half a pound of salt with a quarter of a cup of brown sugar mixed into it. The sugar is what gives the meat its flavor and is also necessary to balance out all the salt you are adding. You will also want to add either a green leafy vegetable such as lettuce or celery or pink salt (otherwise known as Prague Powder #1), which adds sodium nitrite to the curing process to fight off botulism.

Cut your meat into slabs and cover each slab in the salt mixture, then place it in a crock pot or a jar to store, tightly packed together. Store at a temperature around 36 to 38 degrees Fahrenheit for about a month.

Remove the meat and wrap each slab in moisture proof material, such as plastic. You will then want to vacuum seal it and store it in a cool place, preferably your fridge. When you want to use the meat, you can soak it in water to remove the excess salt and then treat it as you would any other meat ingredient.

If this method appeals to you, we recommend purchasing a beginner's guide to curing meats to be sure that you are following the best and safest methods. Cured meats can last several years if the process is approached properly.

Smoked Meats

Meat and fish can be smoked either hot or cold, but will last much longer if the cold process is used. Your smoker won't get hot enough to actually cook the food and the emphasis will be more on drying, so a temperature below 100 degrees Fahrenheit is recommended. Use hardwood or fruit wood chips (make sure you do some research to avoid any toxic varieties if you are gathering wood from your local area). Again, if this method appeals, it's a good idea to find a beginner's guide or a local practical course to be sure you are preserving your meat safely and effectively.

Bottled and Canned Meats

A lot of hunters swear by the bottled meat method and will tell you that it not only frees up space in your freezer, it's also extremely convenient to use, removes the gamey taste from wild meats, can be used for a huge range of recipes and is a smart way to preserve your meat for the long term.

Again, you're going to want to find a beginner's guide or attend a practical course to make sure you are doing this properly, particularly when it comes to sterilizing your equipment and sealing your food containers, but the process is relatively simple.

Replenishing Your Stores

Having access to fresh meats is something we tend to take for granted, and it's not something you need to give up if you find yourself in a situation where you need to fend for yourself. You have two choices when it comes to replenishing your stores: you can either maintain a stock of animals of your own, or make use of the bounty of the land.

Both of these options are going to require some lifestyle changes right now. The first is to keep your own livestock, such as chickens or rabbits, or even a goat or milk cow. If you keep chickens, you'll always have access to fresh eggs, while a goat or cow will provide you with milk. Rabbits can be culled when you need fresh meat for the table. Depending on the amount of land you have available for this project, the same can even be done with pigs.

If your back yard is not up to this task or you live in a city or town where it's not acceptable to keep livestock on your land, all is not lost. Consider taking up one or two outdoor sports; specifically, learn to hunt, fish and trap. This is an important skill in almost any survival situation, so consider it part of your overall training. If you find yourself still off the grid when your storage runs out; if you lose access to your storage for some reason; or even if you simply prefer the idea of supplementing your storage as you go along, this is the ideal way to do it.

If you start now, and find yourself a good mentor to help you learn the basics, you could be an expert hunter, fisherman or trapper by the time you need those skills to survive. You'll also have invested in the equipment needed, such as archery equipment and firearms, traps and snares and fishing equipment. You will feel considerably more confident about your chances of survival when you know you have the ability to bring in more protein whenever it's needed.

Eggs

A fresh egg can be stored for up to four months if properly prepared. This is done by coating the shells in a thin layer of mineral oil, which replaces the coating that it once had when it was laid by the chicken. As mentioned earlier, having a few chickens in your yard can go a very long way towards keeping your protein levels topped up – but you can ensure your household has access to fresh eggs for at least the first few months of your year off the grid by following the mineral oil method.

Obviously, you will want to cycle eggs in and out of your pantry much more quickly than you would other ingredients, so only plan to store as many fresh eggs as you would usually use in a four-month period.

Eggs are a pantry staple, necessary for most baking and popular in a long list of recipes. It would be hard to make it through the rest of the year without access to egg of any kind, so you will also want to consider alternatives.

Powdered Eggs: These are not necessarily easy to find in a supermarket, but can be ordered from food storage companies. This is a great option for your storage for two reasons. The first is the conversion rate: depending on the brand, you can expect one pound of powdered eggs to be the equivalent of around 40 individual fresh eggs. When using your powdered eggs, you will only need a tablespoon (plus the correct amount of water for rehydration) to create the equivalent of one egg. Ordinary powdered eggs have a shelf life of approximately 18 months, but you can extend this to between five and ten years if stored in a cool environment in a vacuum sealed package without oxygen. You can also consider purchasing freeze dried eggs, which can last for up to 25 years and therefore very rarely need to be cycled out of your storage, but bear in mind they will reconstitute as "cooked" egg and therefore won't be usable in baking recipes.

Textured Vegetable Protein

This is usually referred to as "soy meat" and is made from soy flour with the oil removed. Its protein content is comparable to meat and the texture is somewhat similar, but it is absolutely tasteless unless it has been flavored to taste like specific types of meat.

Much TVP has been fortified with vitamins, while it is also high in potassium and essential amino acids. It also includes calcium and magnesium.

Unlike meat, it is dry and has a low bacterial count, and it can also be served to vegetarians. It has a general shelf life of around a year, but this can be extended greatly if it is sealed in an airtight container without oxygen.

TVP can be eaten dry, or rehydrated. Instructions will differ by brand, but will usually involve adding water and cooking for several minutes. TVP is an excellent addition to your storage not only because it will allow you to cook a lot of your favorite meals without the need for meat, but also because it is economical to store and relatively inexpensive to buy.

Nuts and Seeds

Because nuts contain oil, which will go rancid if it's not stored properly, most nuts will only last in your storage for up to one year – and only if you've sealed them properly in a mason jar. However, they are an excellent source of protein, as well as fat and various nutrients.

Always aim to purchase dry roasted and salted nuts, which keep much better on the shelf. It's best to avoid raw nuts as they may contain insect eggs and can also grow fungus – but you can always bake them yourself before storage, if you find a great deal.

Pistachios are perhaps the most nutritious nuts to store, containing plenty of B6 and E vitamins as well as potassium, copper, carotenes, phosphorus and oleic acid. Almonds are also packed with essential nutrients, and will keep for longer than most other nuts if purchased unshelled.

Peanuts, too, contain an extremely long list of nutrients, and will last for months if purchased unshelled. Walnuts are a good source of omega-3 fatty acids but are harder to store than other nuts: if you buy them shelled, check for stains and piercings to be sure they are not developing mold; if you buy them unshelled, they will perish fast unless stored in an airtight container in the fridge.

Cashew nuts and pecans are also viable choices. Pecans store better if unshelled and unprocessed.

Seeds to consider for your storage include sesame, which will stay fresh for months (white seeds should be kept in the fridge), pumpkin, which should be purchased whole, and sunflower seeds, which can be stored at room temperature only if purchased whole.

Another way to store nuts in a way that the family will almost certainly already be familiar with and that will be extremely easy to make use of is in the form of peanut butter. This will usually keep for up to three years in your storage area and can be used for baking, snacking or a lunchtime sandwich.

Beans

Properly stored, dried beans will last up to 30 years with only a miniscule loss of flavor. They are best purchased in already sealed containers and best stored in your five gallon buckets.

With a life span that long, you won't need to worry too much about cycling them in and out of your storage once you've reached your maximum capacity.

The storage time is one excellent reason to include beans in your plans, but it's not the only one. Beans are also relatively cheap while being full of nutrition and extremely versatile for cooking. They are also suitable for vegetarian and vegan members of the family.

You can even use them to replace the fat in your cooking in many dishes, by rehydrating white, black turtle and garbanzo beans and cooking until soft before pounding them with a mallet into the consistency of butter. Prepared this way, they will replace up to half the butter or oil the recipe requires.

There are no beans that store better or worse than other beans, so it's entirely up to you which ones you go for. It's a good idea to research some bean based recipes and give them a go, experimenting with different beans to see which ones you prefer in terms of flavor and taste.

You can also make decisions based on the best uses of certain beans. For example, white beans are often used to make flour for bread and pastries, because their flavor is very mild. Sauce mixes and dried gravy mixes often benefit from soy, lima, pink or mung beans, or lentils and spit peas.

You can, of course, also purchase canned beans, and these are often a tasty accompaniment to meals due to the sauce they are stored in. They can also be easier to use, but bear in mind the shelf life will not be anywhere near as long. These are a better alternative for short and medium term storage.

Grains

Think of almost any meal on your regular menu and you'll immediately realize that one of the foundational ingredients is a carbohydrate. While that can sometimes mean a vegetable, such as potato, it more often involves a grain of some kind – anything from rice to pasta to flour.

Grains are the easiest of this food group to store, often one of the cheaper items to purchase and they aren't just important for meal composition. This category is also our main source of carbohydrates and energy.

Rice

High in calories, this is one of your best available energy sources – especially because rice is one of the most shelf stable options out there. It's filling, allergen free and doesn't contain cholesterol and sodium.

It's also very easy to prepare as it only needs to be cooked from the bag to be ready to eat, and it's an extremely versatile basis for a family meal.

However, rice does need some special considerations for storage: unlike most things on your list, it's going to need to breathe, so it should be stored with some kind of ventilation. A tightly sealed container while actually encourage pests to manifest. Choose food grade plastic containers with lids that are not completely air tight, to allow oxygen to reach the rice. If this isn't possible, you can also use oxygen absorbers. Rice should be stored at 40 degrees Fahrenheit to maximize its shelf life.

Opt for white rice, as this has a longer shelf life than its brown alternative. This is a shame, as brown rice is more nutritious, but the difference is far from negligible. Brown rice can have a shelf life as short as three to six months due to the oil on its outer shell. On the other hand, a bag of white rice stored properly can last you for up to 30 years, making it the ideal basic grain in your pantry because it won't need to be swapped out nearly as often as most of your other pantry ingredients.

Wheat

This is one of the most common grains available in the western world, so you shouldn't have too much trouble sourcing it. You can purchase both soft and hard varieties, with the former most often used for bread and pasta and the latter for pastries.

It's a great addition to your pantry due to the high calorie content, as well as the fiber, protein and manganese contained within it. Like rice, it can also last a long time – up to 25 years when purchased in its basic form.

Unfortunately, there's a downside to storing it in a way that will last a quarter century: the effort required to prepare it. You are also going to need to grind your wheat before using it, and you will need to store leavening and have access to a proper oven. You can purchase hand crank grinders to ensure you are able to process your wheat even in the absence of electricity, but it's a good idea to test out bread and other wheat based recipes to make sure you are able to make use of this ingredient in its raw form.

The good news is that you do have an alternative, though it's ultimately going to prove more expensive. You can purchase various varieties of flour to store, making sure to check the expiry dates carefully. Most flours will last between five and ten years before they go rancid – it's not nearly as long as their raw alternative, but it's still one of your longer life pantry items.

Whole grains should be stored in an airtight container with a tight fitting lid. The material of the container is optional – glass, plastic and aluminum will all work just fine.

Corn

High in protein and carbohydrate, this is another versatile choice for your pantry. You can purchase anything from dent and flint to pod and flour corn, with some varieties vying with rice for its shelf life crown with a storage time of up to 30 years.

Options for corn in your cooking range from the family favorite cornbread to grits and tortillas – it can really add some variety to your cooking. Corn can also be used as biofuel if needed, and to feed any animals you might have on site.

Oats

This is a must have for your pantry, not just for its carb content but also because it's a nutritional powerhouse. Oats are one of the healthiest foods in the world, containing everything from fiber, healthy fats and protein to thiamin, folate, riboflavin, niacin, vitamin B6 and pantothenic acid. It also contains antioxidants and minerals such as phosphorous, magnesium, manganese, iron, potassium, zinc, copper and calcium.

As you can see, you're going to be able to get a whole lot of your daily nutritional needs from just a single bowl of oatmeal in the morning. Even better, oats are extremely filling and easy to prepare, which means they're likely to become your very best friend in the prepper kitchen.

Avoid raw oats in your storage for the simple reason that they require an extreme amount of preparation before they are edible to humans. Instead, go for whole oat groats, which can be cooked in water for about an hour to tenderize and then ground into a rich flour.

Steel cut oats take a little less time to cook at around 40 minutes, while rolled oats and oatmeal are also good alternatives. You might also consider quick cook rolled oats, which will be handy for a meal in a hurry. Instant oatmeal is not usually a good option because the shelf life is considerably lower, but it can still be good to have on hand for a 72 hour kit or for the first days of your isolation. If you enjoy oatmeal in your regular diet and will find it easy to rotate some instant oatmeal in your storage, go ahead and do so. Commercially prepared long term storage oatmeal is also available at specialty locations.

Cans of rolled oats will last for up to 30 years if stored in a cool, dry place and will continue to stay fresh for up to nine months once opened, so make sure to purchase in containers that you can easily get through in a nine month period.

To avoid mold, pests and oxidation, store your oats in an oxygen free environment with low humidity and make sure to seal properly. You can keep the humidity down by using silica gel packets.

Pearl Barley

This grain is a lot less common in regular kitchens, but it appears in more recipes than you might realize. It's a great thickener for soups and stews and is often included in casseroles.

It's a good option because it also contains plenty of nutrients, including lots of fiber, important B vitamins and many essential minerals. It also contains antioxidants and can lower blood cholesterol. It cooks in around 45 minutes in water or a soup, and can also be used to make a porridge.

The shelf life of unopened pearl barley is about ten years. Once open, it will last about 18 months so, again, make sure to purchase in containers you will be able to make use of within that 18 month period.

Pasta

This is an extremely valuable addition to your pantry because it's so easy to prepare and create recipes from. It has a shorter shelf life than most other grain alternatives, but it's still worth investing in – especially as it's not going to be hard to rotate it in and out of your pantry.

Look for the longest possible expiry date on the pasta you buy and bear in mind that it can still be used up to one or two years past this date. You will know it has spoiled if it crumbles, has mold or there's a musty odor to it.

Keep it in the original packaging or use Ziploc bags or mason jars to preserve it. You can extend its shelf life by using a vacuum sealer – this can actually quadruple its time before spoilage.

Other Grains and Seeds

There are endless possible varieties of grains out there on the market, some of which can be substituted for the ones we have already discussed if you or a family member has an allergy or intolerance, such as to gluten. Consider researching the following options to see if you would enjoy the taste or be able to incorporate them into the kind of meals you generally enjoy:

- Buckwheat
- Millet
- Quinoa
- Spelt
- Flax seed
- Kamut grain
- Bulgur wheat
- Amaranth
- Triticale
- Sorghum
- Farro
- Barley

In all cases, whole grains are a better alternative than flour for the sake of shelf life, so do consider storing the equipment needed to process your ingredients. However, flour is still an alternative if you are unable to do this – just be sure to pay attention to the expiry dates. Whether grains or flour, food grade buckets and oxygen absorbers are likely to become your biggest allies in storing your grains.

Oils

This is one of the trickiest categories for a long term storage pantry because most oils go rancid long before you will have a chance to reach the bottom of the jar. Fortunately, there are ways to sidestep this problem and make sure your diet still contains these essential ingredients. With proper storage, oils can last up to five years in your pantry.

The trick to storing oils is to purchase the best quality you can find in the first place. For example, olive oil is better quality than many other liquid vegetable oils, but bear in mind it's also more expensive.

Buy your oils in small containers that can be used in approximately one or two months. Once opened, oil will go rancid more quickly. Make sure to purchase airtight containers and store them in a cool, dark place.

Cooking Oil

A quick glance at the supermarket shelves and you can see what a huge variety of cooking oils are available to you. For the sake of your pantry, the best choice is a hydrogenated oil, which can last up to five years.

Other good alternatives include peanut oil, with a shelf life of up to four years, and olive or palm oil, both of which can stay good for up to three years.

Look for brands with added antioxidants, which are used to protect oils against oxidation and thus extend their shelf life. Oil sprays can sometimes also have surprisingly long shelf lives, so keep an eye out for options that will stay good for a few years.

Butter

Butter powder has a long shelf life of up to ten years if preserved properly in a can, and it can be used in almost any recipe that calls for ordinary butter. That makes it an excellent choice for your pantry, as it will last a lot longer than its fresh alternative.

Canned butter can be even better, especially in terms of taste. It also has a shelf life of ten years with no need for refrigeration, and it has the advantage of not containing preservatives or chemicals.

Ghee and Lard

This alternative to butter is a better option in a survival situation because it can be stored in a cool place for up to a year – or three years if you are able to keep it in the fridge. Lard is a similar situation: you can keep home rendered lard for up to four months at room temperature or up to 18 months in the fridge or a cold root cellar. Look out for commercial lard options, which contain added stabilizers that will allow you to keep it for at least two years at a cool room temperature.

Shortening

Though many families have moved away from shortening in the modern world due to it being a less healthy alternative than other fats, it's still a good choice for your pantry. In an unopened metal can, shortening can last up to five years in your pantry. It's difficult to find in quantities you'll get through in a short period of time, though, so it's worth placing your shortening in sealed canning jars to make the most of the shelf life.

Dairy

You would think that a food group that is generally kept in the fridge and eaten soon after purchase would be impossible to include in a long term storage pantry, but actually there are plenty of alternatives to the fresh and highly perishable milks, cheeses and yogurts that most of us like to eat.

Because dairy products are so vital to baking and cooking, it's important to make sure you have them included in your storage. Fortunately, you won't have to look too hard to find a way.

Milk

There are numerous methods of storing milk that don't involve a bottle in the fridge. For example:

Powdered Milk: You can find this in most supermarkets or purchase in bulk from food storage vendors. Pay attention to the amount of water required to rehydrate the powder as it may affect the amount of water you need to store in your pantry. Powdered milk lasts up to two years.

Long Term Instant Milk: This is an extremely long lived version of powdered milk that will stay good for up to 20 years, meaning that it will be one of those pantry purchases you don't have to worry much about once you have it. It is, however, more expensive than the version you will find in the supermarket. It can be purchased by the bucket or the case.

Condensed and Evaporated Milk: This has a shelf life of about two years and is mixed with water to use for baking and cooking.

Whey Milk: This has a long shelf life and a long list of nutrients. It is best purchased in sealed pouches, to ensure that you are not exposing your entire stock to light, air and moisture every time you access your stock. This, too, can be stored for up to 20 years and can be used for cooking and baking.

Butter

Like milk, this vital ingredient for cooking and baking comes in a variety of different forms. Choose from some of these options to make sure you always have butter on hand, no matter your need.

Clarified Butter: Canned clarified butter is also referred to as ghee, and is usually available in the ethnic food aisle. If you can't find any locally, you can also make your own by heating unsalted butter over a very low heat for 45 minutes without stirring, skimming any bubble scum and then pouring it through a cheesecloth to get rid of the solids. Ghee is a great fat source because the process of making it removes the "bad" cholesterol, and because it can be used to cook at higher temperatures than normal butter. It has a long shelf life and a great taste, and can be substituted for oil or butter in almost any recipe.

Canned Butter: There are various brands of commercially produced canned butter available. It's not a good idea to try this at home, but a purchased version can be a luxurious addition to your pantry and will last a long time while staying stable. It's not cheap, but if you feel like splashing out, it will make for a wonderful treat.

Butter Powder: This does not need to be kept in the refrigerator and the right brand can be used to replace almost any butter application, whether it's a baked good recipe to a sauce or a topping. It isn't as fresh and creamy as real butter but it's great value and versatile. Shop around to find the best brands for your needs.

Cheese

Thinking cheese is surely out of the question for a long term pantry? Think again…

There are ways to enjoy cheese up to a quarter century after it was made, as long as you choose the correct versions. Some of your options include:

Canned Cheese: This really isn't something you can do at home, but you can certainly purchase commercial versions. You can find gourmet cheeses stored in cans that will last for up to 15 years, or canned cream cheese spread that can be used straight out of the can for cooking, desserts and dips.

Freeze Dried Cheese: This product doesn't need to be refrigerated and will melt just like normal cheese once you have rehydrated it. Shelf life varies, but can be up to 25 years with some products. It can also be purchased in a variety of cheese types to add some variety to your diet. It can be used right out of the package or rehydrated using warm water and added to any meal you would normally enjoy with the addition of regular cheese.

Shelf Stable Parmesan: The harder this cheese is, the longer it will last. An unopened can of parmesan will stay good for up to 20 years, while an open can of parmesan will still be usable for up to a year.

Dehydrated Cheese: This can last more than five years in your pantry. It comes in a powdered form, similar to the packets you find in a packaged mac and cheese meal. It can be added to pasta or hot meals, used to make soup, added to potatoes or used with popcorn.

Wax Cheese: If you coat any cheese with a cheese wax and place it on the shelf, it will begin to age and will last up to three months. To do this, melt your cheese wax in a double boiler and dip your cheese into it or brush the wax onto the cheese. The longer it sits on the shelf, the stronger the flavor will get.

Yogurt

You can purchase freeze dried yogurts in many supermarkets, often in forms that are easy to grab for a breakfast or a quick snack. Often marketed towards children, they come in fruity flavors and bite size quantities.

It's also possible to purchase yogurt powders, which last for between one and two years when stored properly. They are produced using pasteurized skim milk that is then cooled to incubation temperature and yogurt cultures are added. Once fermented, it is spray dried and packaged.

These powders have a tart flavor similar to what you'd expect from yogurt and can be used in ways that ordinary yogurt cannot be, such as in coatings for confectionery such as dried fruits. They can also be used in dry beverage mixes to add an extra flavor.

You can also make use of your powdered milk to make your own yogurt by adding freeze dried yogurt starter or acidophilus tablets. This is done by heating your milk to 185 degrees Fahrenheit to denature the proteins and kill bacteria, then allowing it to cool to 110 degrees Fahrenheit and adding your yogurt starter.

The mixture is covered and incubated for between three and 12 hours to set at a temperature between 100 and 115 degrees Fahrenheit. The whey can then be drained or mixed in, flavorings are added and the yogurt will store on the shelf for up to one week.

Miscellaneous Dairy

You may be wondering about other dairy products that, for some of us, constitute a significant part of our normal daily diets. For most of these, you will want to look to powder based alternatives.

These can generally be found via food storage vendors and sometimes through supply stores that cater to restaurants. You should be able to find everything from buttermilk and sour cream to heavy cream in powdered form.

If there are infants in your party, you may also need to store sufficient powdered formula to last for a year. Depending on the age of your baby, you may not need formula for that long and should adjust accordingly. It's important never to use powdered formula past its sell by date, so make sure to shop around to get the best dates for your pantry.

As a side note, if your infant will be transitioning to food soon, you will also want to make sure you have baby foods and cereals in your storage.

Sweets and Sugars

As well as being important for baking and all sorts of family friendly recipes, sweets and sugars help to keep your diet interesting. We all enjoy a good dessert after our meal, right? Sweets and sugars are also a good source of energy – you can pack a whole lot of calories in a single sweet treat, after all.

Sugars

As long as you keep sugar away from moisture, most varieties can be kept on the shelf indefinitely. This is because it resists the growth of microbes and therefore doesn't get along well with molds. It doesn't have nutritional value aside from the calories, but it can sure boost your mood when added to the menu.

Granulated white sugar comes in a range of sizes and should be transferred to tightly sealed containers such as bags, food grade buckets or canning jars. The original packaging will allow it to absorb moisture and clump up – removing oxygen will have the same effect.

Powdered sugar can also be stored indefinitely. Consider purchasing pound or two pound bags and then sealing them in a food grade bucket.

Brown sugar is not as good an option, as it naturally contains more moisture. You can store it for several years, however, so you might want to include at least a few bags in your pantry. In this case, you want to keep the moisture in as much as possible, but the same method of storage will work: put the original bags into food grade buckets.

Honey

Nature's gift to sweet teeth can be kept in containers with tight fitting lids and has an advantage that no other food can boast. Raw honey – the stuff straight from the hive, before it is processed – can actually last forever, so this is the one item you can buy once, place in your pantry and feel confident will be ready and waiting for you whenever you need it. Use it as a sweetener in a wide variety of recipes, eat it as a spread on your homemade bread or add it to a tea for a delicious treat.

Sweet Treats

There are plenty of other sugary options for your pantry, depending on your tastes. Hard candy can last for up to five years, while Twinkies live up to their reputation by storing for up to 30 years. Chocolate doesn't last too long, but cocoa powder can stay stable for up to a decade, which means you can use it to make your own chocolate based treats. Corn and maple syrups also have long shelf lives, which means pancakes are back on the menu, and molasses will last indefinitely. If you do want to store ready made candies and chocolates, make sure to vacuum seal them in a jar, or freeze them if possible.

Beverages

We've already talked about the need to store enough water for each family member, both for drinking and hygiene during your isolation. We've also discussed the need for dairy. But is water and milk the only option you'll have to quench your thirst?

Absolutely not – there are plenty of alternatives that can be stored in your pantry to provide variety to your tastebuds. You just need to keep an eye out for varieties with long expiry dates during your shopping trips.

Avoid bottled or canned drinks, because these can take up a huge amount of your available space and most don't last very long. Aim instead for items you can mix with water to create your beverages.

This includes coffee – whole beans are best in terms of shelf life – and loose leaf teas, as well as hot chocolate mixes, electrolyte mixes and liquid or powdered drink mixes. Take a look at your regular pantry – you might be surprised how long some of those items are able to last.

While most of these choices won't do much for your daily nutrition, some will come with added minerals and vitamins and some are designed to balance your electrolytes. Particularly in the latter case, this can be incredibly handy if a member of your party falls ill from heatstroke, dehydration or other similar issues. Many herbal teas can also be purchased with long shelf lives and many benefits to health.

Consider your beverages more of a treat than an everyday item – water, after all, will see you through.

Fruits and Vegetables

Many fruits and vegetables need to be kept cool in order to last, and almost none will still be good by the end of a year. On the other hand, it's important to get plenty of these ingredients into your daily diet, so produce needs to make up a significant part of your storage. You should be aiming for around one to three cups of fruits and vegetables per day for a child and five for an adult.

There are ways to make some fresh produce last, however, and there are plenty of alternatives for your food pantry to make sure you are getting all the essential vitamins and minerals you need.

Canned Produce

It's easy to find canned fruits and vegetables in your local supermarket and they keep very well in a cool, dark storage space. Canned fruits can last for up to five years and canned vegetables generally stay good for up to three years – check the dates to get the best deal.

These items are a useful addition partly for the pleasant taste and partly because they will not require too much cycling in and out of your pantry. Another advantage is that vegetables are canned after being cooked so, in an absolute emergency, you won't even need to cook them to get some calories and nutrients into your stomach. Fruit that has been canned in its own or additional juice is preferable to heavy syrups.

You can also can your own, home grown fruits and vegetables. Again, invest in a beginner's guide or take a practical course in order to be sure that you are purchasing the correct equipment and using it properly and safely.

You don't need to wait until you are living from your long term pantry and growing your own supplementary produce to start adding home canned produce to your pantry. Consider purchasing produce at a farmer's market or from a nearby grower, or even starting your garden right now. This allows you to control the sugar or salt content and also the variety and mixtures you have on hand.

Dehydrated Produce

You can purchase commercial versions of dehydrated fruits, ranging from apples and blueberries to bananas and apricots. Fruit leathers are also included in this category. You can also dehydrate vegetables to be reconstituted later, and these items will store for up to 20 years.

Again, you will need equipment for this, but it's not as expensive as you might think. You will also need to research your methods to ensure you are dehydrating your foods safely.

Freeze Dried Produce

For fruits and vegetables that will last up to 25 years, and will therefore be easy to store without the need to cycle items in and out of your pantry, consider the freeze dried alternative.

It's more expensive than other options, but freeze dried fruits and vegetables don't require as much storage space and don't have any special needs for storage. The produce will also maintain their nutrients throughout the storage time.

You can also find a great deal of variety in this type of product, which will add some interest to your daily diet. Freeze dried fruits range from peaches, apples, strawberries and bananas to blueberries, pineapple and more. Vegetables include green beans, carrots, onions, broccoli, corn and even mashed potatoes.

Root Cellars

Back in the old days, before refrigerators were invented, many homes used root cellars to store their root vegetables. This includes potatoes, carrots, beets, parsnips, turnips, rutabegas and more.

It's worth considering a root cellar to extend the life of your produce, potentially leading to a situation where you have fresh vegetables available to you at the moment you must begin relying on your long term storage. It's also a good idea if you plan to substitute your pantry by growing your own food, because you'll be able to make it last much longer. It can also be a good place to store your pickled and canned vegetables.

A root cellar takes advantage of the natural properties of the earth, which can cool, humidify and insulate. You will need to be able to maintain a temperature between 32 and 40 degrees Fahrenheit and a humidity level of 85 to 95 percent. This can be done by insulating a section of your basement and building extra walls to enclose it completely. Make sure a ventilation system will bring fresh air in and allow stale air back out to prevent mold.

You can also dig out a root cellar into a hillside or down into the ground. Make sure you have good drainage and aim for sandier soil if possible. An elevated slope will help the water run away from your pit. If the winters are cold in your area, dig deeper to ensure all crops are under the surface of the soil. Line the cellar with straw and dried leaves.

You can even use a garbage can, by digging a hole deep enough for the lid to sit about four inches above the soil level. Heap earth around it, add straw inside the can and cover the lid once full with straw and a sheet of plastic.

With a little research, your root cellar can be used to extend the life of fresh produce if and when you decide to substitute your pantry with home grown fruits and produce.

Dried Fruits

As long as it's stored properly, most dried fruit can be stored for up to a year. If stored in the freezer, they can last for double that amount of time, so there's nothing to stop you from carving out some freezer space for them now, while electricity is no problem, to extend their shelf life later.

Dried fruits come in many varieties, from raisins and cranberries to banana chips. One of the biggest benefits of dried fruit is that all the nutrients and calories have been reduced down into a much smaller package, which means less storage room in your pantry.

Seasonings

It's one of those items that's easy to forget when you're planning a prepper's pantry, but it's also the category you're most likely to regret not having on hand. Seasonings don't just help add variety to your cooking, they also provide vital nutrients for your diet.

Salt

This one is a must-have, for more than one reason. Not only can you keep it stored indefinitely as long as you make sure to keep moisture out of your containers, it's also a vital nutrient for your body. You can purchase boxes and shakers, as well as non iodized salt for canning or pickling. Look out for sea salts and other varieties that are less processed and contain trace minerals to really boost your nutrient intake.

Pepper

This will also last a long time if you purchase in the form of peppercorns – up to four years if stored in a cool dark place. It's one of the most basic and heavily used seasonings in the world, so it's important to have a stash available in your pantry. Again, purchase in smaller containers – this is especially important with pepper, as a little of this spice goes a long way.

Bouillon

Great for soup bases, sauces and much more, you can find bouillon cubes with a long shelf life. Look for the ones with fewer artificial ingredients and aim for better brands, as they will be a worthwhile investment.

Bouillon cubes contain dried and seasoned stock in a range of flavors, from beef and chicken to vegetable and more. These versatile ingredients can flavor almost any meal and can be stored for several years. They're also pretty inexpensive, making them easy to buy, easy to store and, most importantly, easy to use.

Herbs and Spices

In general, whole spices and herbs can be stored in their dried form for up to three years, while seeds, barks and roots last over two years. If you vacuum seal them, they will last even longer – up to several years.

The herbs and spices you choose will be up to you and your tastebuds, but consider investing in a variety just for the sake of keeping your meals interesting over a long period of time. Also bear in mind that some herbs and spices are known to have positive effects on your health; for example, cinnamon is good for diabetics, while cumin is a digestive aid and garlic is packed with antioxidants. A little research on herbs and their applications can go a long way towards building a spice rack that will really benefit your body.

Other good choices include oregano, dill, ginger, rosemary, tarragon, onion, cumin, chili powder, thyme and turmeric. Because it's better to select whole spices for your pantry, you should also invest in a mortar and pestle or a peppermill to grind them before use.

Freeze Dried Herbs

Though not quite as flavorful as fresh herbs and a bit more expensive than dried, this option is a really good idea for at least some of the herbs in your pantry. Why? Because freeze dried seasonings come in little cans with oxygen absorbers that make them shelf stable for up to 25 years.

Conclusion

Your pantry is now full of the kind of foods, drinks and pieces of equipment that will see your family safely through an extended period off the grid. You can feel confident that your nutritional needs have been addressed and that you will survive in relative comfort, no matter how long it takes for civilization to come back online.

There's one final piece of advice to take on board before you put down this book and start buying your ingredients (and, of course, rotating them out on a regular basis.)

Some of the foods in your pantry were probably unfamiliar before you started this project. Some you may have only used a few times, others you've never used before in their raw form, and still others you might not even have heard of.

Before the time comes that you need to make use of all these ingredients, start your own family recipe book. As you rotate items out of your storage, use them together to create meals and snacks that you could replicate in a survival situation.

When you do this, try to refrain from using any other ingredients from your fridge or produce shelf. As often as you can, create new recipes that incorporate as many of the ingredients in your pantry as possible.

There's no point having endless pounds of wheat and oats in your pantry if you don't know what to do with it, after all. When the time comes to make use of your stored food, you will benefit greatly from having a recipe book ready and waiting, full of breakfasts, lunches, dinners and snacks that the whole family has tried and approved.

You'll also find this helps with your regular shopping trips. For example, you'll know that your family enjoys rice more than oats, so you'll be able to weigh your options properly to ensure that everyone's diet is as pleasant – and healthy – as possible.

Within the chapters of this book, you have everything you could need to get started on building, preparing and filling a prepper's pantry. It takes time to complete a project of this magnitude properly, not to mention a significant investment of your finances, so get started right now to make sure you have everything ready when the time comes to use it.

One day, all the work you're about to put into your pantry could make the difference between life and death both for you and for the people you love most. Start small, keep building and watch as your pantry goes from an empty room to a stash that will keep you safe and healthy for as long as it takes to survive.

Special Thanks

I would like to give special thanks to all the readers from around the globe who chose to share their kind and encouraging words with me.

Knowing even just one person found this book helpful means the world to me.

If you've benefited from this book at all, I would be honored to have you share your thoughts on it, so that others would get something valuable out of this book too.

Your reviews are the fuel for my writing soul, and I'd be **<u>forever grateful</u>** to see *your* review, too.

Thank you all!